For Julia,
   When I read this book, I
we know how much you er
and we're sure you might teach someone
else!! Happy Birthday, sweet girl!
       We love you,
    ♥ Nana and Papa Rick ♥

♥ I Love you too! ♥

THE CLIMBING TREE

Barbara Leary

Illustrated by Marrieta Gal

COQUINA PRESS

One summer's day, Eleanor discovered the most amazing climbing tree right in her own yard.

It had been there all along, but she never thought about climbing it until she saw a gray squirrel run across the yard and straight up the tree.

How did the squirrel *do* that?

The squirrel chattered down at her. Did it want to play?

Eleanor stood on her tippy toes and tried to grab a branch, but the branch was too high.

"I'm too little!"

"*Kuk kuk kuk!*" said the squirrel. Was it laughing at her?

The squirrel was not too little to climb the tree. Eleanor was bigger than the squirrel. There had to be a way!

She looked all around the tree until she found a branch she could reach.

Eleanor used her strong arms and legs to climb up to the sturdy branch.

Sitting in a tree for the first time made her feel excited, nervous, and a little wobbly. Eleanor held on tight.

Suddenly, a bee buzzed by. She swatted at it and...
down she fell, all the way to the ground.

Aieeee!

But the next day, Eleanor couldn't wait to climb her tree again. Step by careful step, she climbed up to the sturdy branch. This time, she didn't feel wobbly at all.

Day after day, Eleanor climbed her tree. Her arms got stronger, and her feet knew just where to go. She climbed higher and higher.

Sometimes Eleanor shared her tree with the gray squirrel. She learned not to worry about the bugs. There was room enough in her tree for everyone.

In her tree, Eleanor could pretend to be a pirate sailing the big blue ocean,

or an astronaut flying to the moon,

or a warrior princess riding a winged pony.

Most of the time, she was happy just to be a kid in a tree.

When the weather grew colder, Eleanor watched the gray squirrel gather acorns. So many acorns! She wondered how something
so small could grow
into something
so big and wonderful
as her climbing tree.

One day, Eleanor and her family moved to a new house. She was sad to leave her climbing tree behind. She hugged her tree so hard the bark left little marks on her arms.

A soft breeze blew through the leaves. The branches brushed against her. Eleanor thought she heard her tree whisper, "Goodbye."

"Goodbye," she whispered back.

Eleanor liked her new house, but there were no climbing trees.
No special place for her. She wondered if her tree missed her.
She wondered if it felt lonely too.

One day, Eleanor's mother said, "Come with me. Let's take something to the family that lives in our old house."

A lady and a boy came out to meet them. The lady invited them in. "Won't you stay for tea?"

Her mother went inside, but Eleanor raced off to the climbing tree. Her feet still knew just where to go. Higher and higher she climbed.

She heard a voice call to her from the ground. "Hello up there!" It was the boy.

"Come on up!" she answered back.

The boy just looked at her, like he didn't know how to climb, so Eleanor showed him how to reach the first big branch.

When it was time to go, Eleanor waved goodbye to the boy. Seeing him look happy in the tree made her feel happy too.

"Wait!" The boy's mother gave Eleanor a bag full of acorns. "You can grow a tree in your new yard. We will take good care of this one."

What a gift!
A part of her climbing tree would come with her to her new home.

As a squirrel watched, Eleanor found a special place in her new yard to plant the acorns.

"You can have some of these," Eleanor said to the squirrel. "But leave one for me, and one day we will have the most amazing climbing tree ever!"

For Eleanor Katherine

© 2019 by Barbara Leary

All rights reserved. No part of this publication may be reproduced, stored in a retrieval system or transmitted in any form or by any means, without the prior written permission of Coquina Press LLC.

www.CoquinaPress.com

Hardcover ISBN: 978-1-7340258-0-4
Paperback ISBN: 978-1-7340258-1-1

CPSIA information can be obtained
at www.ICGtesting.com
Printed in the USA
LVHW072155120221
679132LV00010B/299